P9-CCP-919

Who Was
Robert E. Lee?

Who Was
Robert E. Lee?

By Bonnie Bader

Illustrated by John O'Brien

Grosset & Dunlap
An Imprint of Penguin Group (USA) LLC

To David: A real fighter—BB

For my fellow guards on the North Wildwood Beach Patrol—JO

GROSSET & DUNLAP
Published by the Penguin Group
Penguin Group (USA) LLC, 375 Hudson Street, New York, New York 10014, USA

USA | Canada | UK | Ireland | Australia | New Zealand | India | South Africa | China

penguin.com
A Penguin Random House Company

If you purchased this book without a cover, you should be aware that this book is stolen property. It was reported as "unsold and destroyed" to the publisher, and neither the author nor the publisher has received any payment for this "stripped book."

Penguin supports copyright. Copyright fuels creativity, encourages diverse voices, promotes free speech, and creates a vibrant culture. Thank you for buying an authorized edition of this book and for complying with copyright laws by not reproducing, scanning, or distributing any part of it in any form without permission. You are supporting writers and allowing Penguin to continue to publish books for every reader.

Text copyright © 2014 by Bonnie Bader. Illustrations copyright © 2014 by John O'Brien. Cover illustration copyright © 2014 by Nancy Harrison. All rights reserved. Published by Grosset & Dunlap, a division of Penguin Young Readers Group, 345 Hudson Street, New York, New York 10014. GROSSET & DUNLAP is a trademark of Penguin Group (USA) LLC. Printed in the USA.

Library of Congress Cataloging-in-Publication Data is available.

ISBN 978-0-448-47909-5   10 9 8 7 6 5 4 3 2 1

Contents

Who Was
Robert E. Lee?

On January 19, 1807, in
Westmoreland County,
Virginia, Robert
Edward Lee was
born. Robert's father
was Henry Lee. His
nickname was Light
Horse Harry. In the
Revolutionary War, he
was in charge of troops
that rode on horseback.

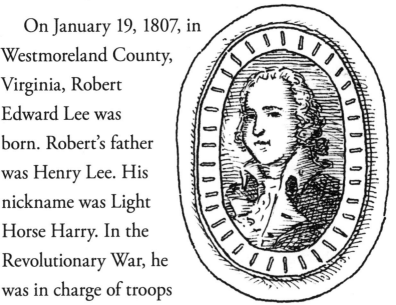

HENRY LEE

He was a strong fighter, a risk-taker, a hero. He
was also a good friend of George Washington.

The Lees of Virginia were famous throughout
the United States. Like Henry Lee, many had

fought in the Revolutionary War. Two of Robert's
cousins were among the signers of the Declaration
of Independence.

Robert grew up with a great love for his
country. Yet, in 1861, the country he so admired
was torn apart by the start of the Civil War.
Robert was torn, too. He wanted the country to
remain united. He did not want the South to
break away from the United States and form a
separate country. But that is what happened.

When asked to lead Northern troops against the South, Robert E. Lee was even more torn. How could he go to war against his friends and family who lived in Virginia? It was a hard choice. Robert thought about loyalty. He thought about honor. In the end, Robert decided to fight against the country that his forefathers helped to create. For Robert the most important thing to him was his family, and his home: Virginia.

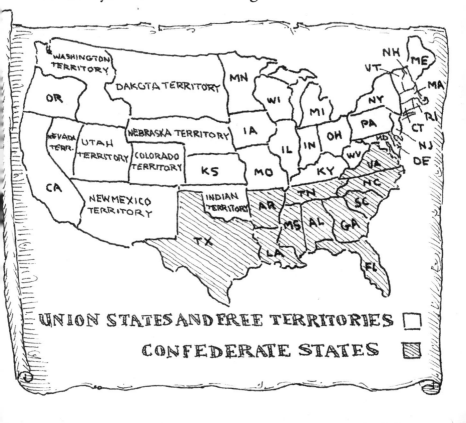

Chapter 1
Lessons Learned

Henry Lee married Ann Hill Carter on June 18, 1793. It was a good match. Ann was young and rich. Her family owned a lot of land near Richmond, Virginia. Henry was the governor of Virginia.

Ann raised Henry's children from his first marriage and gave birth to six more children. Robert was her fifth child. He was named after Ann's two favorite brothers, Robert and Edward.

The family lived in a huge, beautiful brick house called Stratford Hall, surrounded by thousands of acres of land.

By the time Robert was born in 1807, Light Horse Harry wasn't considered much of a hero anymore. He was a gambler. In fact, he landed in jail for owing money to people. There wasn't enough money to keep the plantation running.

PLANTATION LIFE

RICH WHITE PEOPLE IN THE SOUTH LIVED ON BIG FARMS, CALLED PLANTATIONS, WHERE CROPS SUCH AS COTTON AND TOBACCO WERE GROWN. MOST OF THE WORKERS ON THESE PLANTATIONS WERE SLAVES, WHO WERE EITHER BORN IN AFRICA OR DESCENDED FROM PEOPLE TAKEN FROM THERE. THESE SLAVES WERE FORCED TO WORK FOR FREE FROM SUNUP TO SUNDOWN. THE SLAVES HAD NO RIGHTS. AND THE PLANTATION OWNERS GREW RICH.

Upon Harry's release from jail, Ann decided that the family should move from Stratford. She packed the family's belongings and moved to Alexandria, Virginia. Two years later, Henry Lee was badly hurt during a political riot in Baltimore, Maryland. A year after that, Henry decided to go to the West Indies—alone—to recover from his injuries and to try to make money. But he never returned home. On March 25, 1818, Henry died.

Robert was now eleven years old and the man of the house. His two older brothers had left home to start lives of their own. So it was up to Robert to take care of his mother, who was a sickly woman, and his sisters.

Robert loved his mother. She taught him to respect others and love his country. She taught him to be patient. She taught him how to manage money. Above all, she taught him to have faith in God.

As for education, Robert first attended a school for boys that his mother's family had started. He liked to learn and was a good student, although sometimes his teachers thought he was a bit too headstrong!

By thirteen he was a student of William B. Leary's, and then later he attended Benjamin Hallowell's School, in Alexandria. Robert impressed his teachers. He never failed a test. He followed all the rules. He respected his teachers and fellow students.

Soon Robert had to decide upon a career. But what could he do? He did not have a plantation to manage. His mother could not afford to send him to college. Becoming a soldier seemed like the best answer.

In 1823, Robert applied to the West Point Military Academy in New York. It trained young men to become soldiers. It was the best military school in the country, and it was free!

Getting into West Point was not easy. But Robert was recommended by some important people who said that Robert was a good and moral young man.

At last, a letter arrived. The good news was that Robert got accepted to West Point. The bad news was that the class was full. Robert had to wait a year to start.

It was fortunate that Robert's mother had taught him patience. If he had to wait a year, he would!

Chapter 2
West Point

In June of 1825, Robert said good-bye to his siblings and beloved mother. "How can I live without Robert?" she said after he left. "He is both son and daughter to me."

Robert took a train from Virginia to New York. Then he boarded a steamboat and rode up the Hudson River to West Point.

Robert and the other young men entering West Point were called cadets. The life of a cadet was hard. At first they lived in tents overlooking the Hudson. Every day they were up at five thirty in the morning for a full day of classes.

Cadets studied science and math. They also
learned French, since many important military
books and articles were written in that language.
And they learned to draw. Why? So they would be
able to create maps for battle plans.

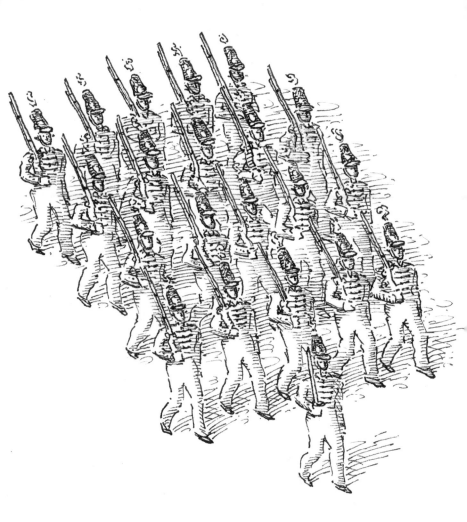

When the cadets were not in class or studying
or taking exams, they performed military drills.
That meant lots of marching! Food was basic—

boiled meat and potatoes, bread and butter. Bedtime was at ten. After living in tents for a few months, the cadets moved to cold stone buildings called barracks. There, they slept on mattresses on the floor.

The young men had little free time and only two full days off: Christmas and New Year's. And there were lots of rules. If a cadet broke a rule, he received a demerit. Too many demerits meant being expelled from school. Among the rules were no drinking, no smoking, no playing cards, no reading novels or plays. But for Robert, the hardest rule was that he could not leave West Point for two years. He could not go home to see his mother.

Robert was so hardworking and so obedient that his classmates called him "Marble Model." By this they meant that he seemed as perfect as a statue made of marble. After his first year, he was named a cadet staff sergeant. This was an incredible honor. And after his second year, as a reward for his excellent performance, he was allowed to visit home.

Sadly, Ann's health had gotten worse. Still, she was well enough to accompany her handsome son on visits to relatives in Virginia.

At five foot ten, Robert was tall for a man of that time. And with his brown eyes and thick black hair, Robert caught the attention of many

MARY ANNE RANDOLPH CUSTIS

young women. One was his cousin Mary Anne Randolph Custis. Robert and Mary had been playmates when they were children.

Mary was the great-granddaughter of Martha Washington, the wife of George Washington, the first president of the United States. Mary's family lived at Arlington House, a beautiful plantation house. There, slaves worked the land.

ARLINGTON HOUSE

All too soon, Robert's visit to Arlington came to an end. It was time to return to West Point.

ROBERT E. LEE'S VIEWS ON SLAVERY

ROBERT GREW UP WITH SLAVES WORKING THE LAND THAT HIS FAMILY OWNED. SOME HISTORIANS SAY THAT ROBERT WAS AGAINST SLAVERY, AND THAT IS WHY HE CONSIDERED FIGHTING FOR THE NORTH DURING THE CIVIL WAR. HOWEVER, OTHER HISTORIANS SAY THAT ROBERT DID NOT OBJECT TO SLAVERY. ONE HISTORIAN UNCOVERED LETTERS WRITTEN BY ROBERT SAYING THAT HE SAW SLAVES AS PROPERTY, THAT HE OWNED THEM AND THEIR LABOR. ROBERT THOUGHT THAT THE ONLY ONE TO DECIDE TO FREE THE SLAVES SHOULD BE GOD.

Robert worked hard for the next two years. In 1829, he graduated second in his class from West Point (and without any demerits).

All graduates of West Point must serve in the United States Army. Robert decided to join the military Corps of Engineers. As an engineer, Second Lieutenant Lee would help build bridges, roads, and railways in the United States. Robert was eager to begin work. But first, he wanted to go home to see his mother.

Chapter 3
Love and War

Only a month after Robert returned home, his beloved mother died. It was July 26, 1829. What should have been a happy reunion turned into a time of terrible grief. Ann Hill Carter Lee was fifty-six years old.

While in Alexandria, Robert paid several visits to Mary Custis. Robert enjoyed Mary's company. She was not pretty and did not dress well, but she was charming, smart, and interesting to be around. In time, the two fell in love.

In August, Robert received orders to report to Cockspur Island, Georgia, by the middle of

November. His job was to design and help build
the foundation of a fort—Fort Pulaski—on the
marshy and isolated island. The work was hard
and dirty. Day after day, Robert waded through
thick muddy water to survey the area and sketch
the details of the early construction. He was cold
and wet and tired. But he wanted to do a good job

on the project. Robert's commanding officer was impressed with his determination and sense of duty.

At every opportunity, Robert paid visits to Mary in Virginia. On one visit, he asked her to marry him. She said yes. Like his father, Robert

was about to marry into a very rich and important family.

On June 30, 1831, Robert and Mary were married at Arlington House. Mary moved with Robert to Fort Monroe, Virginia, where he now worked as an engineer. But Mary did not like living there. She missed her big and beautiful home. After Mary gave birth to their first child, Robert sent her back to Arlington House.

On September 16, 1832, George Washington Custis Lee was born. He was the first of seven children that the Lees had: Mary Custis Lee, born July 12, 1835; William Henry Fitzhugh Lee, born May 31, 1837; Anne Carter Lee, born July 1, 1839; Eleanor Agnes Lee, born February 27, 1841; Robert E. Lee Jr., born October 27, 1843; and Mildred Childe Lee, born February 10, 1846.

Because of the army, Robert was away from his family a lot. He supervised the building and improvement of many forts in the United States.

Forts were important because they protected the American people who were settling new land farther west. At that time, many people were afraid of attacks by Indians. Robert traveled to places such as Fort Calhoun, which was on the land that later became the state of Nebraska; Fort Hamilton in New York; and Fort Macon in North Carolina. He also worked on building piers and waterways in places like St. Louis, Missouri. But Robert was often bored, and he found the paperwork that came with his jobs to be absolutely frustrating!

The separations from his family were hard for Robert. Sometimes Mary and the children went with him on assignments. Other times they stayed home. Robert was a good and loving father. He enforced a strict code of behavior—a code that none of the children dared to disobey! But he also liked to play and joke with his children and gave some of them funny nicknames. George was "Boo," Mary was "Daughter," Eleanor was "Wigs," Robert Jr. was "Brutus," and Mildred was "Precious Life."

On May 13, 1846, just a few months after the birth of the Lee's last child, the United States declared war on Mexico. Robert had been a soldier for seventeen years, but now, for the very first time, he was going to war.

Robert's first post was with the engineering staff in Texas. This job was more of what he had been doing for so long. He helped build and repair bridges and roads in Texas—six hundred miles in all!

Then Major General Winfield Scott, one of the commanders of the US Army, asked Robert to be a scout. A scout's job was to figure out the best route for troops to take to reach the enemy and attack. Sometimes

MAJOR GENERAL
WINFIELD SCOTT

scouting meant getting very close to enemy lines. Robert had to be careful not to get caught!

One day, Major General Scott had a plan to surprise Mexican troops in an attack. He sent Robert ahead to check the best route to take.

Robert set out and found a path to the enemy, when suddenly he heard Spanish voices! Quickly, he hid behind a log and covered himself with bushes. He could hear the Mexicans coming closer and closer. Someone stepped right over the log he was hiding behind.

THE MEXICAN-AMERICAN WAR

IN 1845, TEXAS BECAME THE TWENTY-EIGHTH STATE. FORMERLY, PARTS OF TEXAS HAD BELONGED TO MEXICO, AND MEXICO DID NOT WANT TO GIVE UP CONTROL OF THE LAND. THE RESULT WAS WAR.

AMERICAN TROOPS MARCHED INTO MEXICO. ON MARCH 29, 1847, AMERICAN MAJOR GENERAL WINFIELD SCOTT'S UNIT CAPTURED THE CITY OF VERACRUZ. THEN IT WAS ON TO MEXICO CITY. ONCE THE CITY WAS CAPTURED, THE FIGHTING ENDED.

ON FEBRUARY 2, 1848, BOTH SIDES SIGNED THE TREATY OF GUADALUPE. IN THIS AGREEMENT, MEXICO GAVE UP TEXAS, CALIFORNIA, UTAH, AND NEVADA, AS WELL AS PARTS OF ARIZONA, NEW MEXICO, WYOMING, AND COLORADO. FOR ALL THIS, THE UNITED STATES PAID MEXICO FIFTEEN MILLION DOLLARS.

Robert remained calm and perfectly still until the Mexicans were gone. He reported back to his camp. General Scott was pleased with Robert's news. He ordered his soldiers to move ahead to attack.

During his service in the Mexican-American War, Robert proved that he was smart, strong, loyal, and brave. His commanding officers took notice. They saw that Robert E. Lee was someone to keep their eye on—a future leader.

Chapter 4
Back to West Point

With the Mexican-American War over, Robert returned to Arlington House. He had been away from home for almost two years. Even though he was just forty-one years old, his face was creased with wrinkles. His hair was turning gray. The Lee children stared at him—this was not the father they remembered!

The family was happy to be together again. On July 3, 1848, Robert was given a job in

Washington, DC. The capitol was only a few miles away. He was to redraw maps to include the land won in the Mexican-American War. For the next few years, Robert was able to work jobs that were close to home.

When his eldest son was about to start his third year at West Point, Robert received a surprising job offer. He was asked to become superintendent—or head—of West Point! Robert wasn't sure that he was the right man for the job. The people at West Point had more confidence in Robert than Robert had in himself!

In the end, Robert agreed to take the position. The Lees moved to West Point. There they would spend the next three years. As soon as Robert arrived, he saw that changes needed to be made. Cadets weren't being taught the proper classes. There were not enough horses for the students to ride. Buildings were run-down. Robert worked hard to fix all of this.

By the end of his time there, much progress had been made. Most rewarding to Robert was the time he spent with students. Each week he invited some of them to dinner at his home. Robert was a great role model for the cadets.

Custis graduated West Point first in his class.
Following in his father's footsteps, he, too, took a
job with the Corps of Engineers.

In March of 1855, Robert's time at West Point came to an end, too. A new assignment came: lieutenant-colonel in the Second Calvary at Camp Cooper, Texas. His job was to keep the settlers in the new state safe from attacks by Apache and Comanche people. Robert was not happy living in Texas. It was hot and dusty. And once again, he was away from his family. But as always, he did his duty.

Then in 1857, word came from home. Mary's
father had died. Robert rushed back to Arlington
House. When he got there, he discovered that
Mary was ill. Very ill. She could not walk. Robert
had to push her in a wheelchair.

Robert took leave from the army. Not only did
he have to take care of his sick wife, he had to take
care of his father-in-law's house. He was now also
in charge of the slaves that worked the land.

The issue of slavery had divided Americans
since the Founding Fathers wrote the Constitution
and created the government of the United States.
There were heated arguments in Congress,
and among ordinary citizens, about what to do
regarding slavery. Those who wanted to end
slavery were called abolitionists. (To *abolish*
means to end something.)

John Brown, a preacher from Connecticut, was a fierce abolitionist. As he grew older, his ideas about how to end slavery grew more and more radical. Slavery was so evil, Brown believed, it was not wrong to use violence to end it. In 1856, John Brown and his sons killed five white pro-slavery men in Kansas. From then on, he was a wanted man.

JOHN BROWN

Brown believed that hundreds of slaves would join him in a rebellion against their white owners. The slaves would need weapons. So on October 16, 1859, John Brown, along with a band of twenty-one men, including two of his sons, captured an armory in Harpers Ferry,

Virginia, and took hostages. An armory is a place
where weapons are stored.

Members of the local Virginia militia soon had the armory surrounded. They demanded that John Brown surrender and free the hostages. John Brown refused and moved the hostages to the small engine house next to the armory.

What now?

An order was sent to Lieutenant Colonel Robert E. Lee, who was on leave nearby in Virginia. Robert had to take charge of the situation. Under his command, the militia and the US Marines stormed the engine house in Harpers Ferry. Ten of John Brown's men were killed. Seven were arrested, including John Brown, who was later hanged for his crime. In the South, Robert E. Lee was seen as a hero.

But in the North, many considered John Brown a hero. Some historians even go so far as to say that his failed rebellion sparked the Civil War. Once blood had been spilled over slavery, there was no stopping it.

Chapter 5
A Terrible Choice

Robert was fifty-four years old in 1861. He had many successes in his life. Everyone who knew him loved him, from his wife and children, to the men he served with in the Mexican-American War, to the students at West Point. He was smart, brave, and respected. Everything he did, he did well. People looked up to him. In troubled times, they looked to him for answers.

One question he had difficulty answering was whether the United States should remain one country. The issue of slavery was dividing North and South. The United States had a new president: Abraham Lincoln. And he was firmly against slavery.

Virginia, Robert's home state, and many other

ABRAHAM LINCOLN

Southern states were now threatening to secede—leave—the United States. They would create their own country where slavery would continue without interference from the North. Robert knew that secession would lead to war. Lincoln would not just sit back and let the United States be broken apart. On January 23, 1861, Robert wrote, " . . . I can anticipate no greater calamity for the country than a dissolution of the Union . . . and I am willing to sacrifice every thing but honor for its preservation."

Three weeks after this letter was written, Robert was asked to report to Winfield Scott in Washington. In March, the two men met and talked for three hours. They probably discussed the turmoil the country was facing. A little later on, at the request of Abraham Lincoln, Robert was asked to lead one of the Union's field armies. That would mean fighting against the South. Robert was a conflicted man. Clearly, he had a lot to think about. He spent time with his family at Arlington. He prayed. He stayed up late at night pacing the floors.

In the end, Robert reached an answer. He would resign from the US Army that he had served for thirty years. Although he said he would never bear arms against the Union, his heart was with Virginia. He had to defend his homeland.

So, Robert became a citizen of a new government that had formed by the seceded states: the Confederate States of America. Jefferson Davis, who formerly had been a US senator from Mississippi, became president.

Many people were shocked at Robert's decision, especially those in the North. Some called him a traitor.

JEFFERSON DAVIS

As a man of honor, and a Virginian, Robert felt he had no other choice. In a letter to his sister, Ann Lee Marshall, he wrote, "With all my devotion to the Union and the feeling of loyalty and duty of an American citizen, I have not been able to make up my mind to raise my hand against my relatives, my children, my home."

Lincoln knew there was no way to stop the war from coming. However, Lincoln did not want the North to start the fighting. In South Carolina there was a fort—Fort Sumter—that housed Northern soldiers. On April 12, 1861, Southerners attacked the fort and the Northern troops were forced to surrender. The Civil War had begun!

Many Confederates thought the war would end quickly with a Southern victory. Robert thought differently. He knew that the North was strong— it had more money, more weapons and supplies, and more men to form into an army. It would be a long and terrible war.

FORT SUMTER

On April 22, 1861, Robert left his home at Arlington and rode his horse to Richmond. There, the governor of Virginia asked Robert to lead Virginia's army and navy. Robert said yes.

Robert had a big job ahead of him: organizing his state for war. He called for volunteer soldiers. Men eagerly reported for duty. But these were not the type of soldiers Robert had fought with in Mexico, or helped to train at West Point. No. These were ordinary people. Farmers and local townsfolk. Some wanted to fight to protect their families and their homes. Others were just looking for adventure. All of them were ill-prepared for war.

Chapter 6
The Fight Begins

By May 1861, Robert had been promoted to brigadier general in the Confederate army. In the first months of the war, he served as an advisor to Jefferson Davis. Robert quickly proved his talent for understanding how to win battles.

On July 21, word came that the first major battle of the war had broken out near Manassas Junction, Virginia. The battle, known as the First Battle of Bull Run, raged for five hours. At first it looked like the Union troops were going to win. But then extra Southern troops were ordered to the battlefield—an order issued by Robert. With the reinforcements, the Confederates were able to win.

Planning battle strategy was not the same as being in the thick of the fight. Robert was

not happy sitting on the sidelines. He wrote to
his wife saying, "I wished to partake in the . . .
struggle, and am mortified at my absence."

Then, in September, Robert not only got to
plan but command his first battle. It was at Cheat
Mountain in West Virginia. Robert's plan was
for three different units of Confederate soldiers
to surround the mountain and attack the Union

army at the same time. It was a smart battle plan. The fog hung low over the mountain, and rain fell from the sky. The Confederate soldiers were unfamiliar with the rocky terrain. Still, they marched on. But then the commander of the first unit decided not to follow Robert's plan and did not attack.

It was a bad decision. The Confederates ended up losing the battle.

In newspaper accounts of the battle, Robert was blamed unfairly. People called him "Granny Lee." They said he was too afraid to attack.

It was a hard time for Robert. He felt ashamed. Also, conditions for the soldiers were bad. The weather was turning colder. Rain fell. There were no tents. Many men didn't even have coats. Robert had a coat and a tent, yet he could not sleep at night as his men shivered.

The Union enemy still loomed on the other side of the mountain. Again, Robert launched an attack. But this failed, too.

Robert was "carrying the heavy weight of defeat," Jefferson Davis wrote. "And unappreciated by the people whom he served, for they could not know, as I knew, that, if his plans and orders had been carried out, the result would have been victory rather than defeat."

Robert's next job was to protect the coastline along South Carolina, Georgia, and Florida.

Robert did what he knew best from his years as an engineer: He oversaw the construction of forts along the coastline. Big guns were put into place, ready to face the Union army if—and when—an attack came.

It was now Christmas of 1861, and once again Robert was away from his loved ones. In the past, Robert took comfort knowing that the rest of his family would be together in their beautiful Arlington home. But not this year. The Union army now occupied the Lees' former house. Mary, suffering from arthritis, and her four daughters stayed at various plantations belonging to relatives, trying to find a permanent home.

It was a difficult time in Robert's life. So far, he had proved that he was better behind the scenes than on the battlefield. But he longed to *fight*, to help the South win the war—even if it was a war he hadn't believed in.

Chapter 7
A Great Leader

The war was not going well for the Confederates. The Union soldiers were threatening Southern forts on the eastern coast. Farther west, the Confederates lost battles in Tennessee and Kentucky.

Once again, Robert was called back from the field to serve as President Davis's advisor. "I have

been placed on duty here to conduct operations under the direction of the President," Robert wrote to Mary. "It will give me great pleasure to do anything I can to relieve him and serve the country, but I do not see either advantage or pleasure in my duties. But I will not complain, but do my best."

Then disaster struck—Confederate General Johnston was wounded during a battle at Shiloh, Tennessee. Who could take his place?

Robert E. Lee.

Robert was asked to take charge of the Army of Northern Virginia in June 1862. Yet people knew very little about him as a fighter. Sure, he was smart behind the scenes, but up until now, his record on the battlefield had been poor.

This was just the opportunity that Robert had been waiting for. He was determined to prove to the people of the South that he could lead the way to victory. He set up headquarters about two miles

from Richmond. When he walked in, the other
officers were stuck by his good looks. His hair
was now gray, and he had grown a beard. Dressed
in a simple gray uniform with his pants tucked
into his riding boots, Robert flashed his white
teeth and broad smile. He looked every inch the
commanding general.

Robert first wanted to make sure that
Richmond, the Confederate capital, was safe from
the Union armies. He ordered his men to pick
up spades and dig trenches around the city. The
trenches would serve as shelters for Robert's men
in case the enemy attacked.

UNION GENERAL
GEORGE McCLELLAN

Some in the Confederacy did not approve of this defense work. They called Robert "King of Spades." Why was he digging instead of attacking? Union General McClellan and his army were marching closer and closer to Richmond.

When McClellan was only eight miles from Richmond, Robert held a meeting with his top generals. They decided they could no longer just defend the city. It was time to go on the offensive—to attack the Union army.

The battles that followed were known as the Seven Days' Battles because they lasted a week. The first one took place on June 25 at Oak Grove, Virginia. For several days there was no clear victory for either side. Then, taking about fifty-four thousand men, Robert attacked the Union soldiers at Gaines's Mill.

The battle was fierce. Many lay injured or dead on the battlefield—over four thousand on the Union side, and over seven thousand Confederates. In the end, the Confederates were victorious. And Robert E. Lee finally was recognized as a tough fighter—a brilliant and aggressive general, a man who was willing to take risks.

Under Lee, the Army of Northern Virginia had become one of the strongest units fighting in the Civil War. Northern troops feared and respected Lee and his men.

Robert determined it was time to move farther north into enemy territory instead of fighting on Southern soil. The men's spirits were up; the Confederate soldiers now thought they had a chance of winning the war. Robert put three men in charge of his soldiers. General "Stonewall" Jackson and

GENERAL "STONEWALL" JACKSON

GENERAL JAMES LONGSTREET

General James Longstreet were to each command a group of soldiers who fought on foot and who handled the big guns. General James (Jeb) Stuart was to command the cavalry: soldiers on horseback.

On August 30, the Confederates racked up another victory at the Second Battle of Bull Run.

Robert kept his army on the move. They marched across the Potomac River into Maryland, a slave-owning state that had remained in the Union. By now Robert's men were tired.

GENERAL JAMES (JEB) STUART

Food was scarce. Uniforms were wearing thin. But

Robert did not want to stop to rest. Some soldiers ran away. They were too hungry and too scared to go on. The entire Army of Northern Virginia was down to just fifty-five thousand men.

Robert decided to split his army into two
groups. One would stay near Frederick, Maryland.
General Jackson would lead the other group to
Harpers Ferry, Virginia. But Northern soldiers
found a copy of Robert's plans. This could have
been a disaster for the Confederates. But it wasn't.
Why? Union General George McClellan waited

too long to attack. His mistake gave the
Confederate army more time to get ready.

As the sun rose on the morning of September
17, McClellan sent some of his troops to attack the
left side of the Confederate army. Then he sent
some soldiers to the right. McClellan hoped this
plan would leave the center of Robert's army open

to attack. McClellan's soldiers charged.

Sitting on top of his horse, Traveller, Robert watched the battle from high up on a hill. Puffs of white smoke from the cannons covered the field. Men on horseback and soldiers on foot charged

against the Northern army. Robert was proud. His troops fought hard. They were brave. They worked as a team—something that McClellan's men did not do. By the end of the fight, the Battle of Antietam, Robert lost 2,700 men. Another 9,024 were wounded, and two thousand were missing or captured. The Northern army had big losses, too. In all, over twenty-two thousand men were either dead or missing. It was the bloodiest day in the Civil War so far.

As night fell, Robert's men remained on the battlefield. They wanted to prove their toughness. But they were tired and hungry, and there were just too few of them left to fight another day. So Robert ordered his army to retreat back to Virginia. To win the war, he had to have more men.

Chapter 8
A Fighter to the End

Robert moved the Army of Northern Virginia to Opequon Creek, Virginia. He wanted to give his men a short rest and then engage McClellan's army in battle again.

Robert pleaded with Jefferson Davis to send food and supplies. His men needed warm clothing. And shoes. Davis sent what he could, and Robert rounded up more men, growing his army to about eighty thousand.

Robert's duty was to his men, so even when his daughter Annie died in October, Robert really had no chance to grieve. There were more battles to fight.

In an effort to hasten the war's end, President Lincoln issued the Emancipation Proclamation on September 22, 1862. This order stated that all the slaves in the Confederate states were free as of January 1, 1863. Lincoln's hope was that newly freed slaves would rise up against their former owners and help the Northern soldiers.

GENERAL
AMBROSE E. BURNSIDE

Lincoln also chose a new top general, General Ambrose E. Burnside, to replace McClellan, who, in Lincoln's opinion, did not fight as hard as Lee. In December, a Union army 120,000 men strong marched toward Fredericksburg, Virginia. Burnside bombarded the town. Houses were set on fire. People ran for their lives. At first it looked as if the Union soldiers were going to capture Fredericksburg. But then the course of the battle turned around. Looking down from his post on a hill, Robert saw thousands of men—his men—in gray uniforms rushing down toward the Union soldiers who charged up the hill.

In the end, Robert's army pushed the Union soldiers out of Fredericksburg. But it was not enough of a victory for Robert. He wrote to Mary, "[The enemy] went as they came, in the night. They suffered heavily as far as the battle went, but it did not go far enough to satisfy me."

In January 1863, General Burnside began to move his troops toward Fredericksburg again. But the roads were covered with mud, and they

couldn't pass. Robert knew they wouldn't march again until the roads cleared in the spring.

Both sides had to wait out the cold of the winter. The weather was hard on Robert and his men. The railroads in Virginia were so worn out that it was difficult to get supplies to the army. There was not enough food for the men or for the horses. And there was a shortage of artillery supplies, too.

In April, Robert caught a bad cold. He had pains in his chest. He had a fever. His entire body ached. Doctors told him to rest, but he didn't have much time to recover. Northern troops were on the move.

This time, it was the Battle of Chancellorsville. Although the Confederates were victorious, Robert suffered a great, and personal, loss. His greatest fighter, General Jackson, was accidentally shot by one of his own men during the battle. Robert, who was not on the battlefield at the

time, wrote to him saying, "I have just received your note informing me that you were wounded. I cannot express my regret at the occurrence. Could I have directed events, I should have chosen for the good of the country to have been disabled in your stead." A week later, Stonewall Jackson was dead.

In June, Robert decided to try once again to take control of the North. Confederate troops crossed the Potomac River on their way to Pennsylvania. Robert's men were hungry, but he forbade them to steal food from stores or homes. They had to pay for whatever they took.

On July 1, Robert's men were met at
Gettysburg, Pennsylvania, by the Union forces.
The Battle of Gettysburg lasted three days. In
the end, Southern troops were forced to retreat
back to Virginia. It was a huge defeat for the
Confederacy and for Robert. His strategy had not
worked.

The Battle of Gettysburg was a turning point in the war. It soon became clear that, brave as the Southern troops were, the Confederate army was outnumbered. Defeat was inevitable.

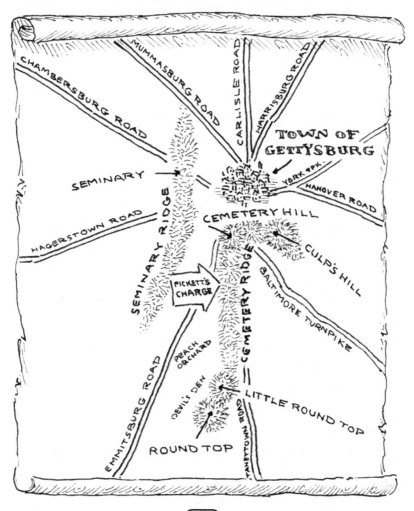

THE BATTLE OF GETTYSBURG

GEORGE PICKETT

THE BATTLE OF GETTYSBURG TOOK PLACE OVER THREE DAYS IN GETTYSBURG, PENNSYLVANIA. THE FIRST DAY, THE CONFEDERATES FORCED THE UNION ARMY TO RETREAT TO CEMETERY HILL. ROBERT ORDERED ONE OF HIS GENERALS TO GO AFTER THE UNION ARMY, BUT THE GENERAL REFUSED. THIS GAVE THE UNION ARMY TIME TO STRENGTHEN THEIR FORCES WITH ADDITIONAL TROOPS FROM MARYLAND. ON THE SECOND DAY, ROBERT'S ORDERS WERE NOT FOLLOWED ONCE AGAIN. THE UNION ARMY HELD THEIR LINES. ON THE THIRD DAY, CONFEDERATE GENERAL PICKETT AND 12,500 MEN CHARGED STRAIGHT TOWARD THE UNION SOLDIERS. THIS ATTACK, KNOWN AS PICKETT'S CHARGE, WAS A DISASTER—ALMOST A SUICIDE MISSION. THE BATTLE OF GETTYSBURG WAS THE DEADLIEST BATTLE IN THE CIVIL WAR. THE ARMY OF NORTHERN VIRGINIA SUFFERED TWENTY-EIGHT THOUSAND CASUALTIES. THIS MEANS THE SOLDIERS WHO DIED, WERE WOUNDED, OR WERE MISSING IN ACTION. THE UNION ARMY SUFFERED TWENTY-THREE THOUSAND CASUALTIES.

Robert blamed himself for the horrible loss at Gettysburg. Once again, he began to question his ability as a general. Was he the right man to lead the army? Also, his health was not good. Robert never fully recovered from his cold, and he was plagued by arthritis. Riding Traveller was hard and painful. Robert wrote to Jefferson Davis. He asked to be replaced. He thought a younger man would do a better job. Davis said no.

Robert worked harder than ever. He stayed up late at night. He looked at maps. He reviewed battle plans. He knew he had to continue the fight. It was his duty. But the situation was only getting worse. Men were starving. Many died from disease. Of those who survived, some deserted. And the Union army kept on getting stronger.

In March 1864, in yet another change of leadership, Lincoln put Ulysses S. Grant in charge of the entire Union army. At last the North had the general it needed to defeat the South. Like Robert, Grant had gone to West Point. He also had fought in the Mexican-American War. Unlike Lincoln's previous generals, he was not afraid to fight. His goal was to destroy the Army of Northern Virginia. In a telegram to another general, Grant summed up his strategy: "Wherever Lee goes, there you will also go."

ULYSSES S. GRANT

ULYSSES S. GRANT NEVER WANTED TO BE A SOLDIER. BUT HIS FATHER SENT HIM TO WEST POINT TO GET A GOOD EDUCATION. AFTER HE GRADUATED, HE FOUGHT IN THE MEXICAN-AMERICAN WAR, THEN HAD OTHER POSTS IN THE ARMY. BUT HE WAS UNHAPPY. HE MISSED HIS FAMILY. HE STARTED TO DRINK. HE QUIT THE ARMY. THEN WHEN THE CIVIL WAR STARTED, HE REJOINED. THE WAR CHANGED GRANT. IT BROUGHT OUT A TOUGHER MAN.

HIS FIRST VICTORY CAME WHEN HE CAPTURED FORT DONELSON IN TENNESSEE IN FEBRUARY 1862. THIS WAS ALSO THE FIRST MAJOR VICTORY FOR THE UNION ARMY. HE THEN ATTACKED THE CONFEDERATE CITY OF VICKSBURG, MISSISSIPPI, IN 1863. IN 1864, PRESIDENT LINCOLN MADE

ULYSSES S. GRANT

GRANT THE COMMANDER OF ALL UNION ARMIES, AND THE NORTH WON THE WAR IN APRIL OF 1865. IN THE YEARS AFTER THE WAR, GRANT SERVED TWO TERMS AS PRESIDENT, FROM 1869 TO 1877.

On September 2, 1864, Grant's second in command, General William T. Sherman, captured Atlanta. On December 16, Union General George H. Thomas defeated the Confederate army at Nashville, Tennessee.

It was now April 1865. The Confederacy suffered its biggest blow yet. The capital of the Confederate States, Richmond, fell. The Union army raised the American flag. Robert and his army fled west to the town of Amelia Court House, Virginia. He thought he would find much-needed supplies there. But the Union army prevented that. Robert was stuck. What now?

His decision was to move on. Robert and his men marched all day and all night. They met the Union army near the town of Appomattox Court House in Virginia. Weak from lack of food and sleep, Robert's men fought on. At first, it looked as though they'd win. But in the end, this was another defeat.

At camp, a letter arrived for Robert. A letter from Ulysses S. Grant. Grant asked Robert to surrender. Here was another terrible decision Robert had to make. Still, he knew what had to be done. It was time to give up. "I suppose there is nothing for me to do but go see General Grant," Robert told an aide. "And I would rather die a thousand deaths."

On the morning of April 9, 1865, Robert put on a special gray Confederate uniform. He buttoned his shirt, picked up a long jeweled sword, and put it in his scabbard. Then he pulled on his boots and placed a gray felt hat on his head. Off he rode on Traveller to meet Grant. "If I am to be General Grant's prisoner today," he said, "I intend to make my best appearance."

But he was not taken prisoner. The two generals met in a house in the small village of Appomattox Court House. They sat down at a table and faced each other. Grant was dressed as an ordinary soldier, wearing a blue flannel blouse and boots splattered with mud. The men talked for over two hours. Grant agreed to let all the Confederate soldiers go home. And they could keep their horses and personal weapons. Robert agreed to disband his army. He signed a document surrendering. The war was over. The Confederacy had lost. All the states that had seceded now had to return to the Union. Just as before 1861, there would again be one country: the United States of America.

Robert rode back to his men. "I have done what I thought was best for you," he told a group of soldiers. "My heart is too full to speak, but I wish you all health and happiness."

The next day, as rain fell, Robert mounted Traveller and rode home to Richmond. All along the way, his disbanded army rushed to greet him. Wild cheers rang out—cheers of love and respect for the man who had been their leader.

Chapter 9
The Last Years

Robert returned to Richmond for a happy reunion with his family. But the Lees had lost a lot during the war. Their home was gone. Robert and Mary's daughter, daughter-in-law, and two grandchildren had died. Robert was sick. He had

chest pains. It was painful to walk. His family had no money. Robert desperately needed a job.

Then news came that rocked the entire country. On April 14, President Lincoln was shot.

By the next morning, he was dead. Robert was shocked. And sad. Andrew Johnson was sworn in as president.

Robert's personal troubles continued. He was charged with treason by the US government.

ANDREW JOHNSON

This serious crime means someone has been disloyal to the government and has tried to destroy it. Robert asked to be cleared from the charges. He did not want to go to trial. He did not want to land in jail. No one would agree to this until General Grant stepped in and helped get the charges of treason dropped.

Next Robert tried to get back the rights of a US citizen that he had lost when he joined the Confederacy. Robert signed a paper pledging his loyalty to the United States and sent it to the secretary of state. Unfortunately, Robert's letter was lost. He never heard back and thought his request for citizenship had been denied. That was not the case. The letter wasn't found until over a hundred years later! In 1975, the United States Congress passed a law that gave Robert back his citizenship.

Robert knew that he had to get on with his life. But what could he do? Joining the army was not possible. Maybe he could buy a piece of land. But a farmer's life was not for him. He also thought about writing a book about his role in the Civil War. Then he received a letter from Washington College in Lexington, Virginia.

The college wanted Robert to become its president! The college was small. The salary was just fifteen-hundred dollars a year. Even though that wasn't a lot of money, Robert was honored and surprised. He did not think he was the right man for the job. However, he had run a school before: West Point. Robert thought about it more and accepted.

WASHINGTON COLLEGE, LEXINGTON, VA

In September, Robert rode Traveller to
Washington College. The school had just four
teachers and forty students. Robert worked
hard to enlarge and improve the school. He
wanted students to be able to pick their classes.
He encouraged the students to take courses in

journalism, engineering, Latin, and math. He knew many of the students by name and was loved by all.

A year after Robert joined Washington College, four hundred students had enrolled. Robert continued to make improvements. And that was satisfying. Yet he could never leave the war completely behind.

Several times during the next few years, Robert was called to Washington. He was asked questions about the Confederacy. The government wanted to bring charges against Jefferson Davis.

Robert continued to work hard as college president. But his health was getting worse, and so was Mary's. By the summer of 1868, it was hard for Robert to ride Traveller. His body ached. His heart was weak.

By March 1870, Robert had to take a leave from the college. He needed a rest. Along with his daughter Agnes, he traveled throughout the South

by train. Crowds of people greeted him. He posed
for pictures. He shook hands. All the time,
he felt sicker and weaker.

When the new school year came around,
Robert returned to work at Washington College.
But he could only walk very slowly. His shoulders

drooped. Then, on September 28, 1870, he lost the ability to speak.

Robert spent the next week in bed, surrounded by family. Sometimes he opened his eyes. He tried

to nod when asked a question. But mostly, he slept. He did not want any medicine. Or food.

At nine thirty in the morning, on October 12, 1870, Robert E. Lee died.

Robert E. Lee spent most of his life as a soldier. Yet, it is important to remember that he hated war. To Mary he wrote, "What a cruel thing is war, to separate and destroy families and friends . . . to fill our hearts with hatred instead of love for our neighbors, and to devastate the fair face of this beautiful world!"

TIMELINE OF
ROBERT E. LEE'S LIFE

1807	Robert Edward Lee is born on January 19 in Westmoreland County, Virginia
1825	Leaves home to attend US Military Academy at West Point
1829	Graduates second in his class from West Point
1831	Marries Mary Custis at Arlington House
1852	Accepts a job as the superintendent of West Point
1855	Moves to Texas to serve as a lieutenant colonel in the Second Cavalry
1859	Involved in stopping John Brown's raid at Harpers Ferry
1861	Offered command of the Union army, but declines Resigns from the US Army
1862	Takes charge of the Confederate Army of Northern Virginia
1863	President Abraham Lincoln issues the Emancipation Proclamation, freeing slaves in Confederate states The Battle of Gettysburg marks a huge defeat for the Confederacy
1864	Ulysses S. Grant takes charge of the Union army
1865	On April 9, Robert meets with General Ulysses S. Grant in Appomattox Court House to surrender Becomes president of Washington College in Lexington, Virginia
1870	Dies on October 12

TIMELINE OF
THE WORLD

The size of the United States doubles when France—— **1803**
agrees to sell land in the Louisiana Purchase

Fighting begins between the United States and—— **1812**
Great Britain in the War of 1812

The Missouri Compromise establishes slavery-free—— **1820**
territory in the United States

Mexico becomes a republic and prohibits slavery—— **1824**

William Lloyd Garrison establishes an antislavery—— **1831**
newspaper called *The Liberator*

Slavery is banned in the British Empire—— **1833**

Texas declares independence from Mexico—— **1836**

The United States declares war on Mexico—— **1846**

Former slave Frederick Douglass creates an—— **1847**
antislavery newspaper called *The North Star*

The Mexican-American War ends—— **1848**

Harriet Tubman escapes to freedom—— **1849**

Harriet Beecher Stowe's *Uncle Tom's Cabin* is published—— **1851**

Abolitionist John Brown's raid fails—— **1859**
in Harpers Ferry, Virginia

Abraham Lincoln is elected sixteenth president—— **1860**
of the United States

Confederate States of America formed—— **1861**
Civil War breaks out between North and South

The Thirteenth Amendment to the US Constitution—— **1865**
ends slavery in the United States

The Fifteenth Amendment to the US Constitution—— **1870**
gives black men the right to vote

BIBLIOGRAPHY

Arnold, James R. and Roberta Weiner. **On to Richmond: The Civil War in the East 1861-1862**. Minnesota: Lerner Publications Company, 2002.

Benoit, Peter. **The Surrender at Appomottox**. New York: Scholastic, 2012.

Eicher, David J. **Robert E. Lee: A Life Portrait**. Dallas: Taylor Trade Publishing, 1997.

Gradowski, Patricia A. **Robert E. Lee: Confederate General**. Philadelphia: Chelsea House Publishers, 2001.

Pryor, Elizabeth Brown. **Reading the Man: A Portrait of Robert E. Lee Through His Private Letters**. New York: Penguin Books, 2007.

Rosenberg, Aaron. **The Civil War**. New York: Scholastic, 2011.

Trudeau, Noah Andre. **Robert E. Lee: Lessons in Leadership**. New York: Palgrave Macmillian, 2009.